Amazing Picture Book of

Monet

This book belongs to…

So teach us to number our days, that we may apply our hearts unto wisdom.

Psalm 90:12

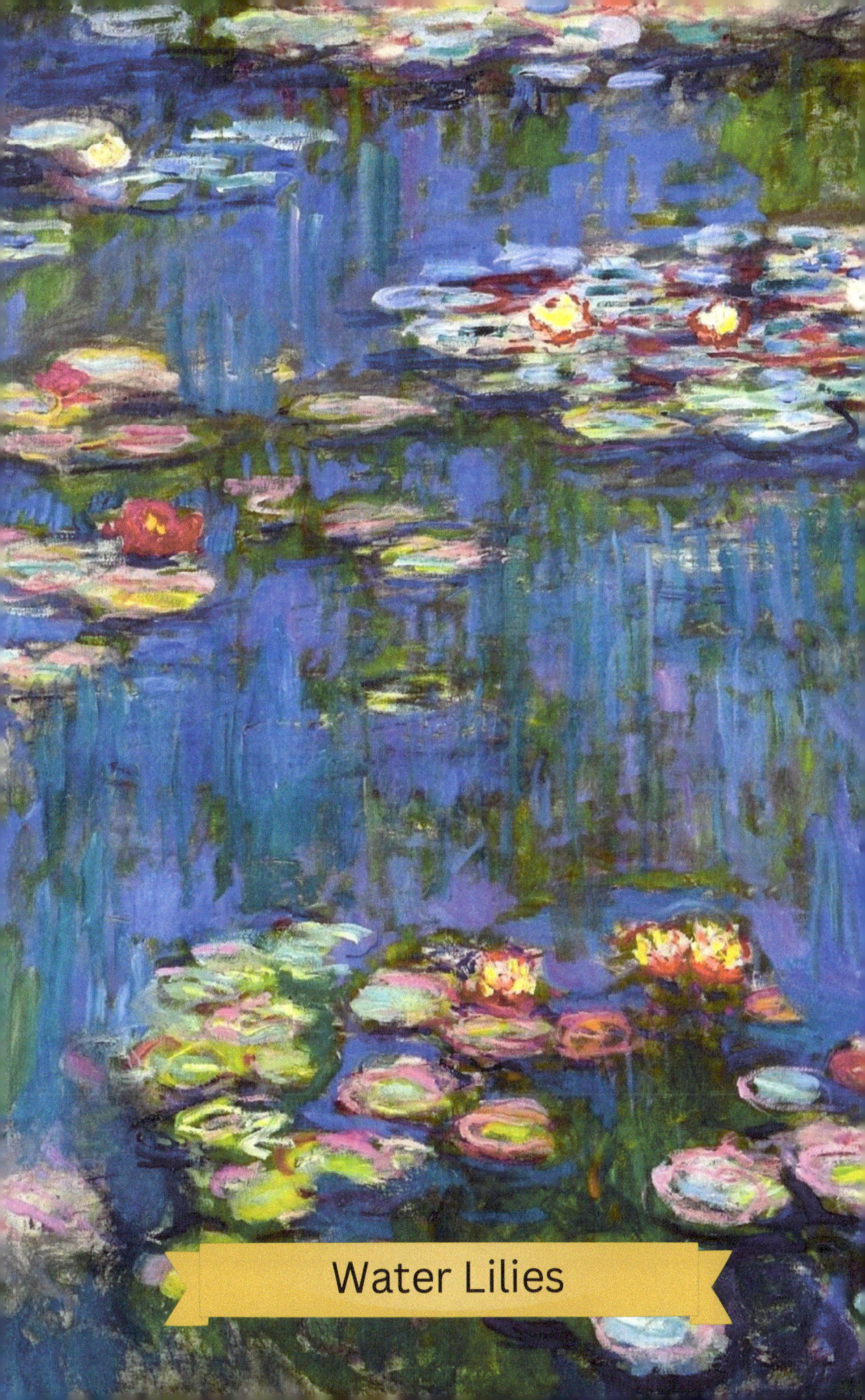
Water Lilies

Yes, my soul, find rest in God; my hope comes from him.

Psalm 62:5

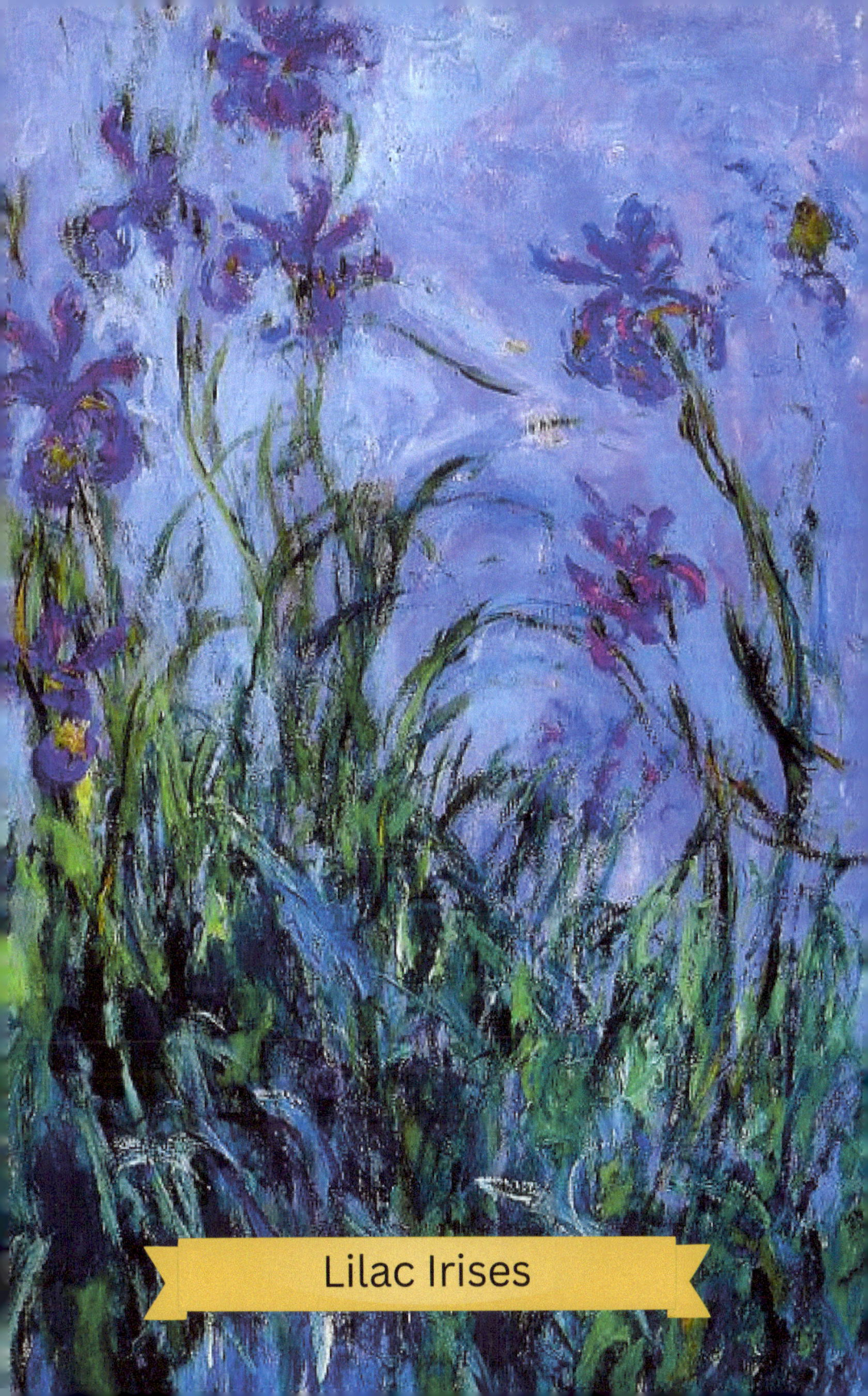
Lilac Irises

Let the peace that comes from Christ rule in your hearts.

Colossians 3:15

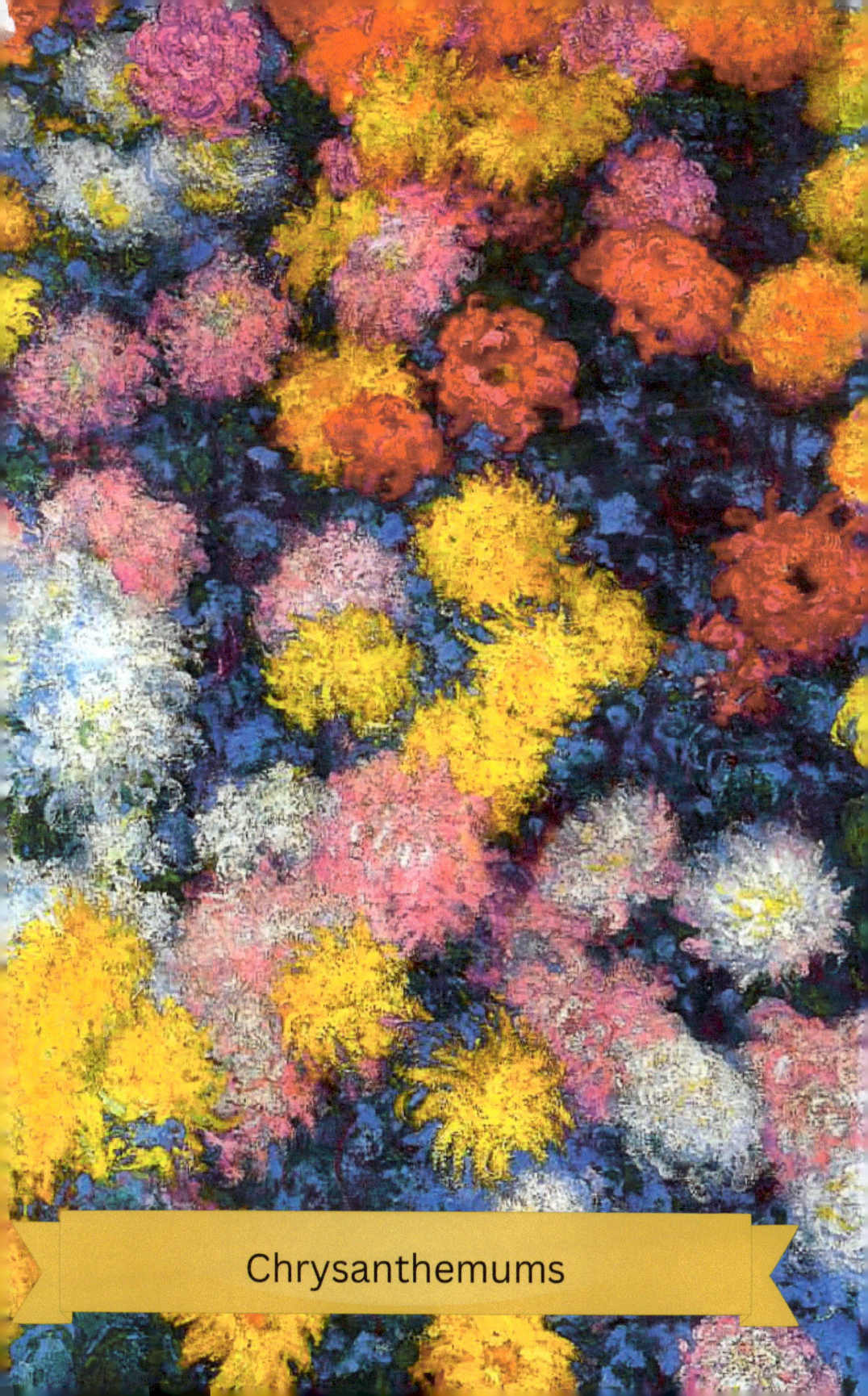

The LORD bless you and keep you;
the LORD make his face shine on you and be gracious to you;
the LORD turn his face toward you and give you peace.

Numbers 6:24-26

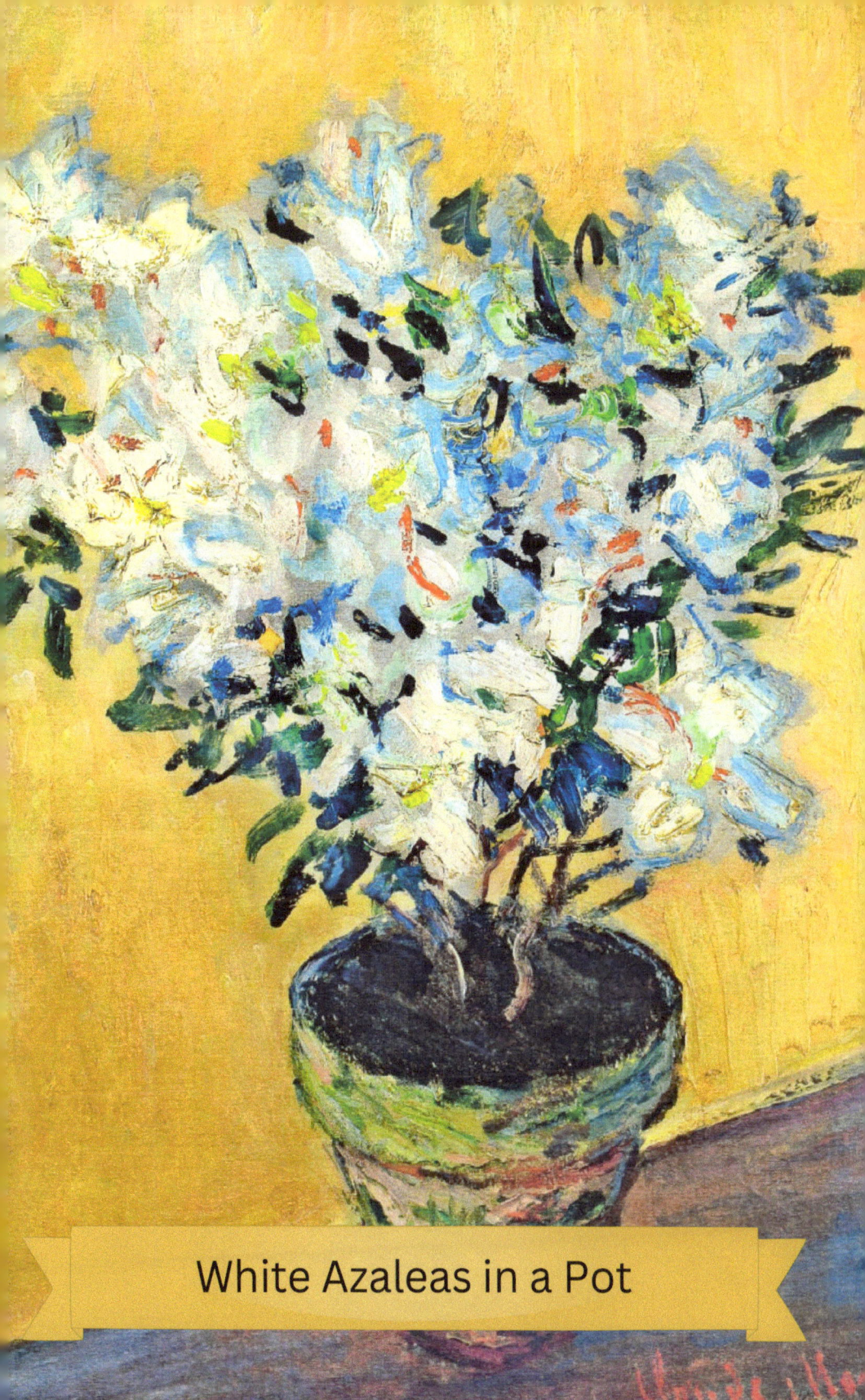

White Azaleas in a Pot

**The LORD will keep you from all harm—
he will watch over your life.**

Psalm 121:7

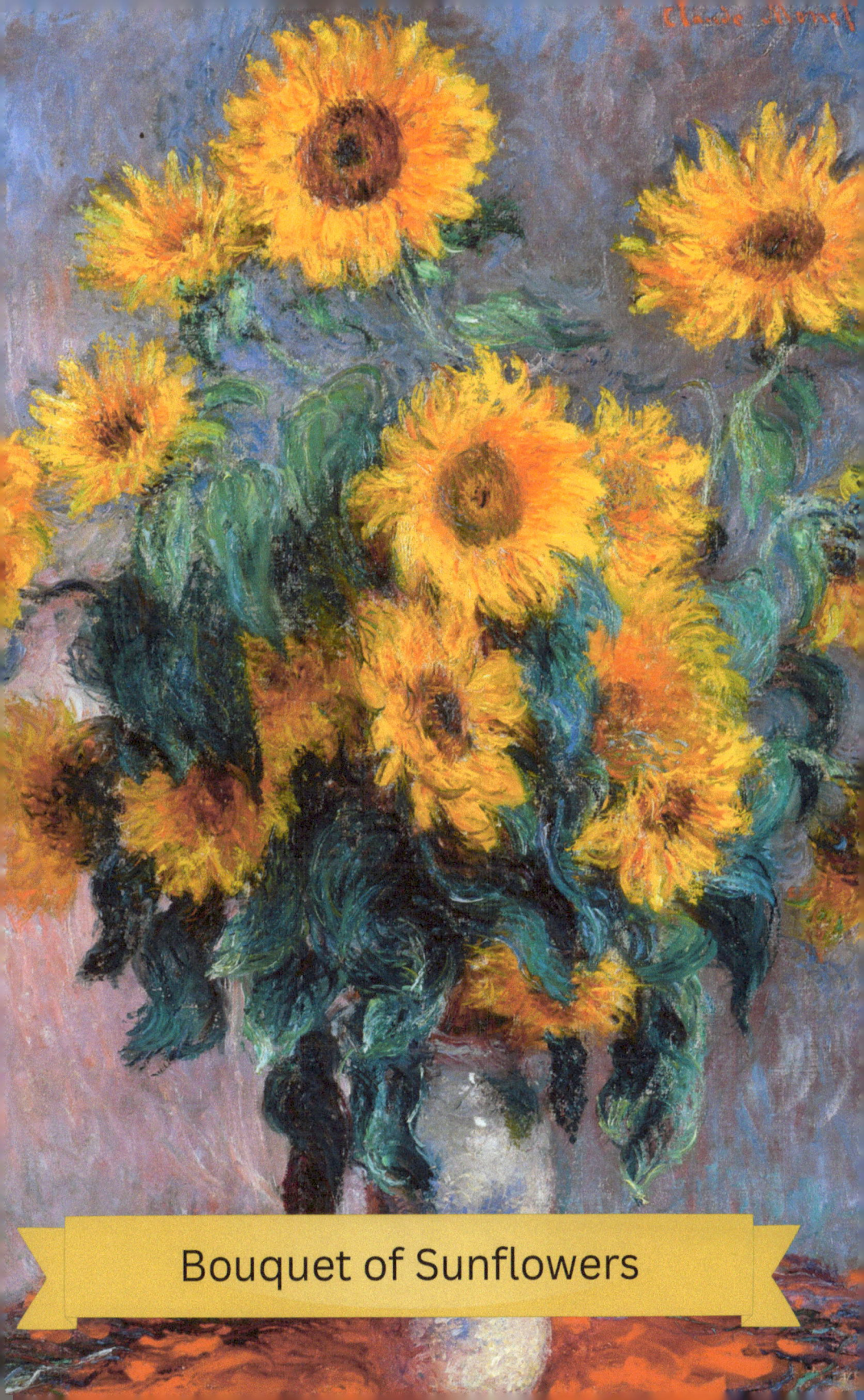
Bouquet of Sunflowers

Be completely humble and gentle; be patient, bearing with one another in love.

Ephesians 4:2

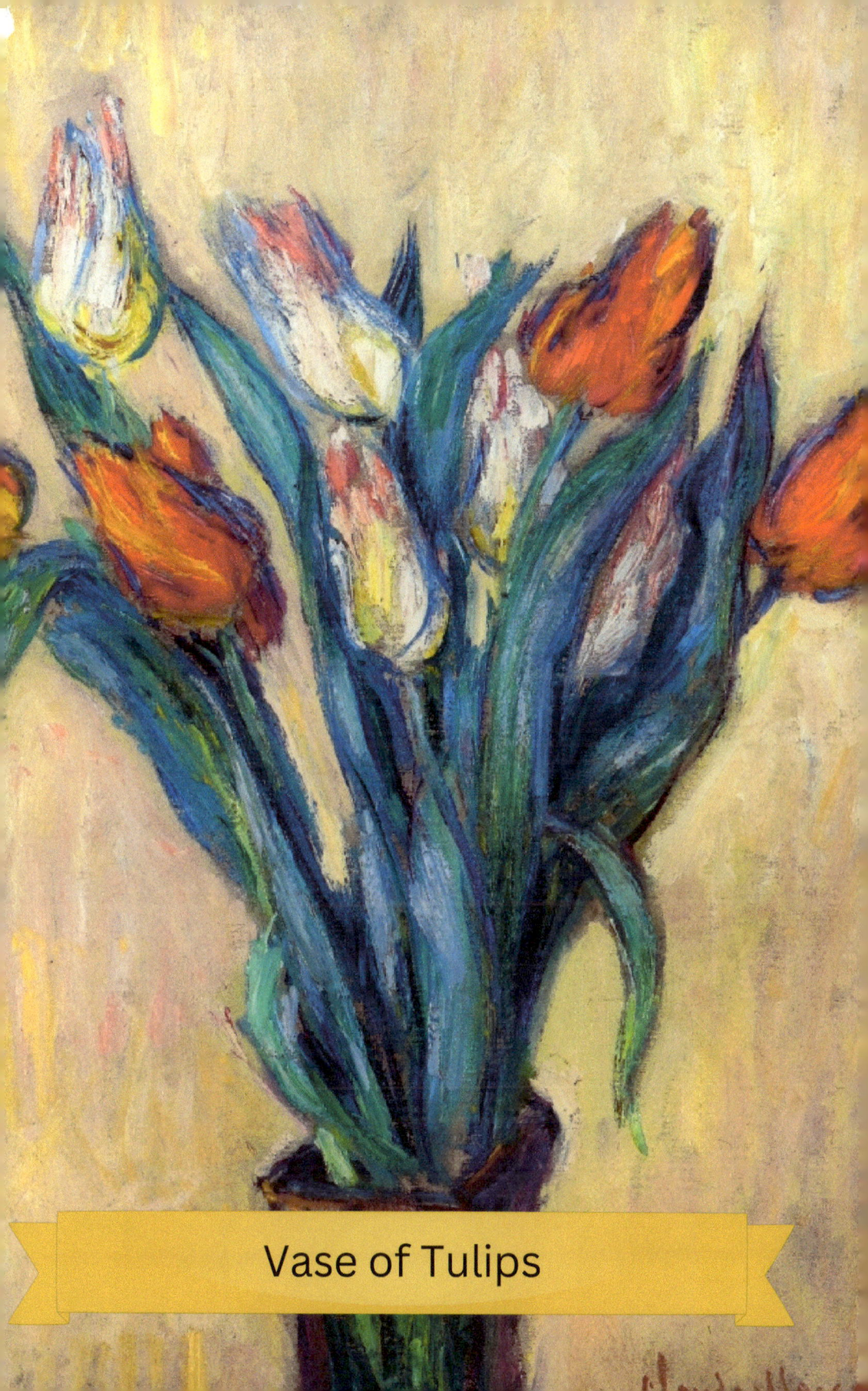
Vase of Tulips

Worship the Lord your God, and his blessing will be on your food and water. I will take away sickness from among you.

Exodus 23:25

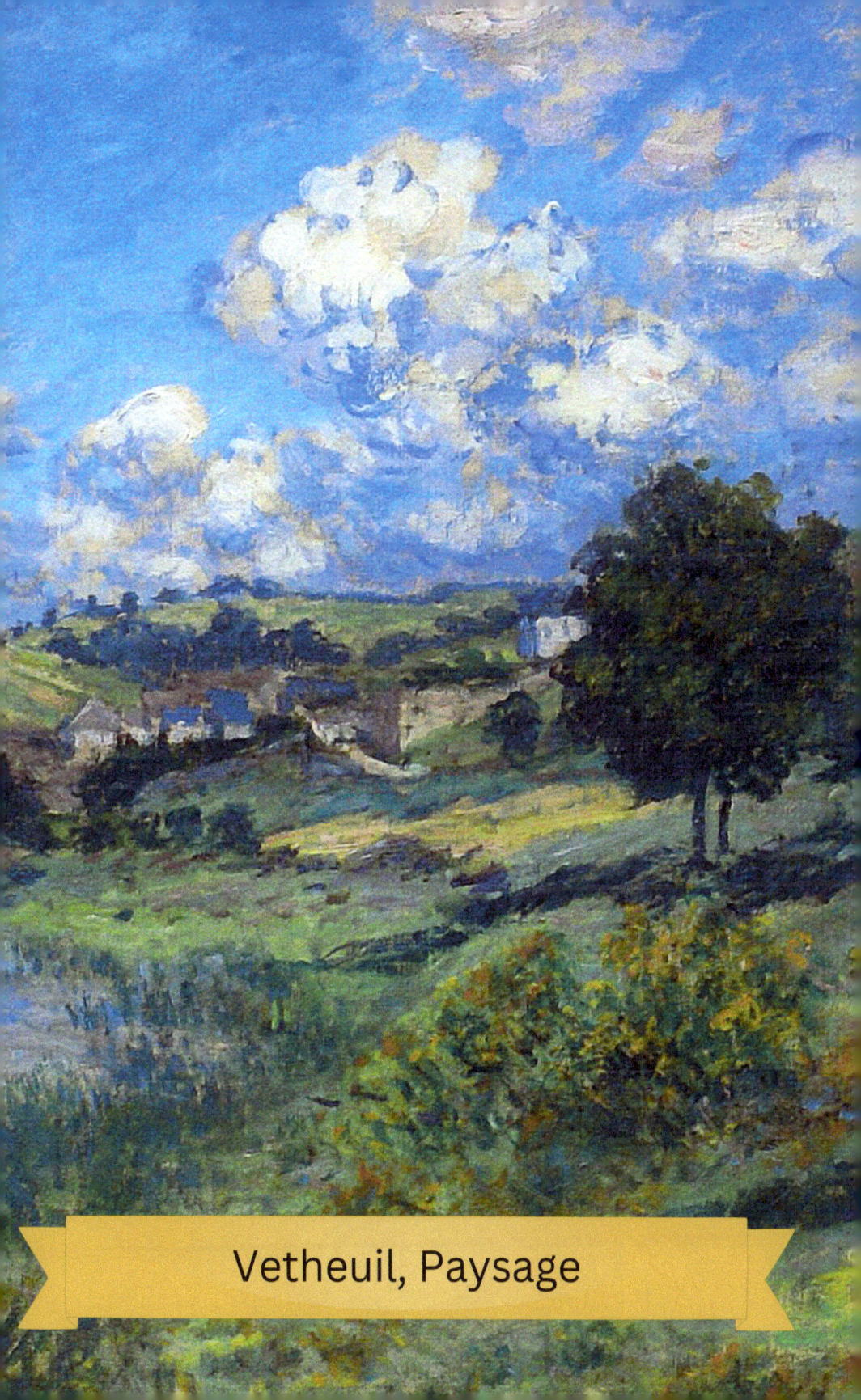
Vetheuil, Paysage

Let love and faithfulness never leave you;
bind them around your neck,
write them on the tablet of your heart.
Then you will win favor and a good name in the sight of God and man.

Proverbs 3:3-4

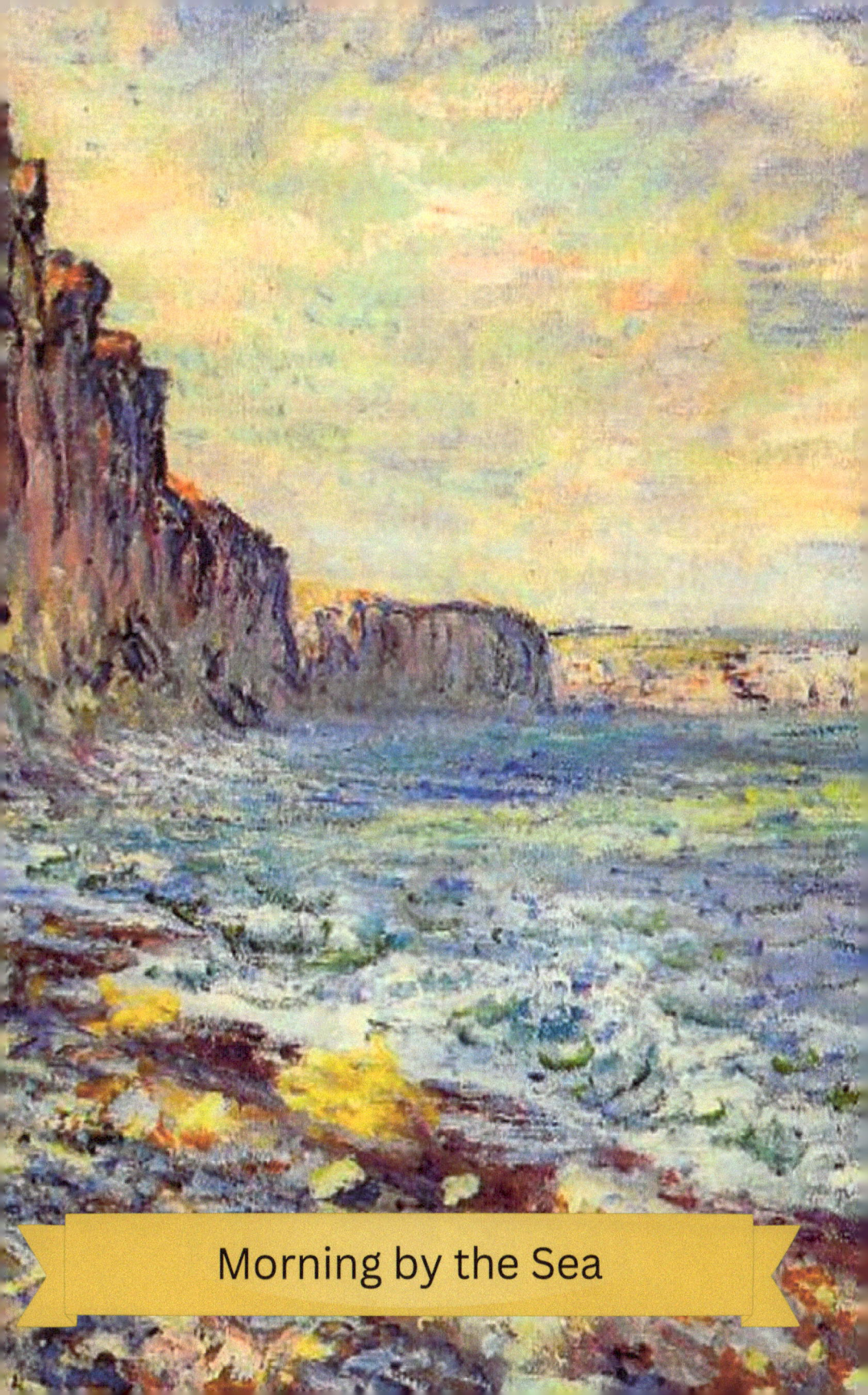

Morning by the Sea

When I am afraid, I put my trust in you.

Psalm 56:3

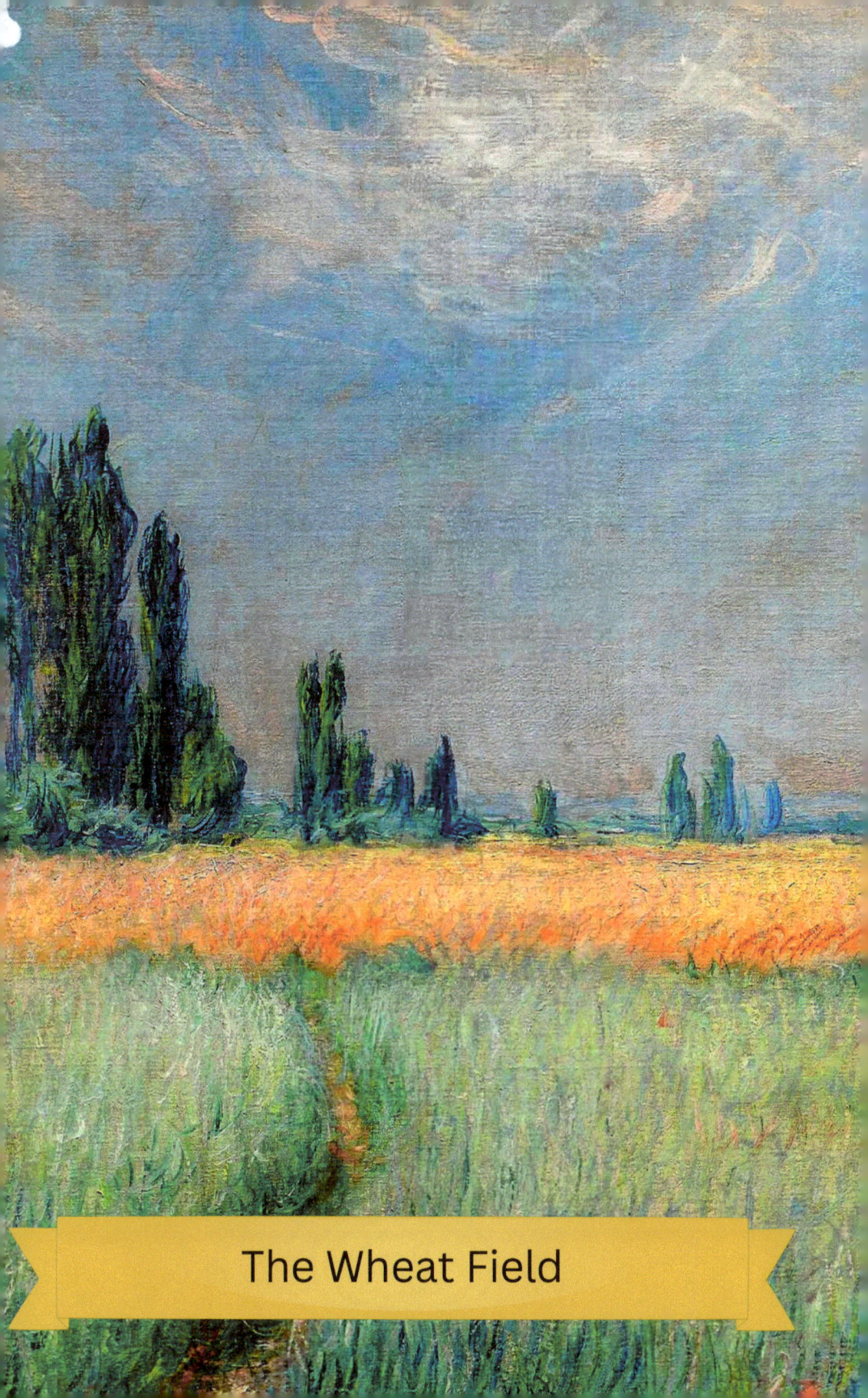

The Wheat Field

Be joyful in hope, patient in affliction, faithful in prayer.

Romans 12:12

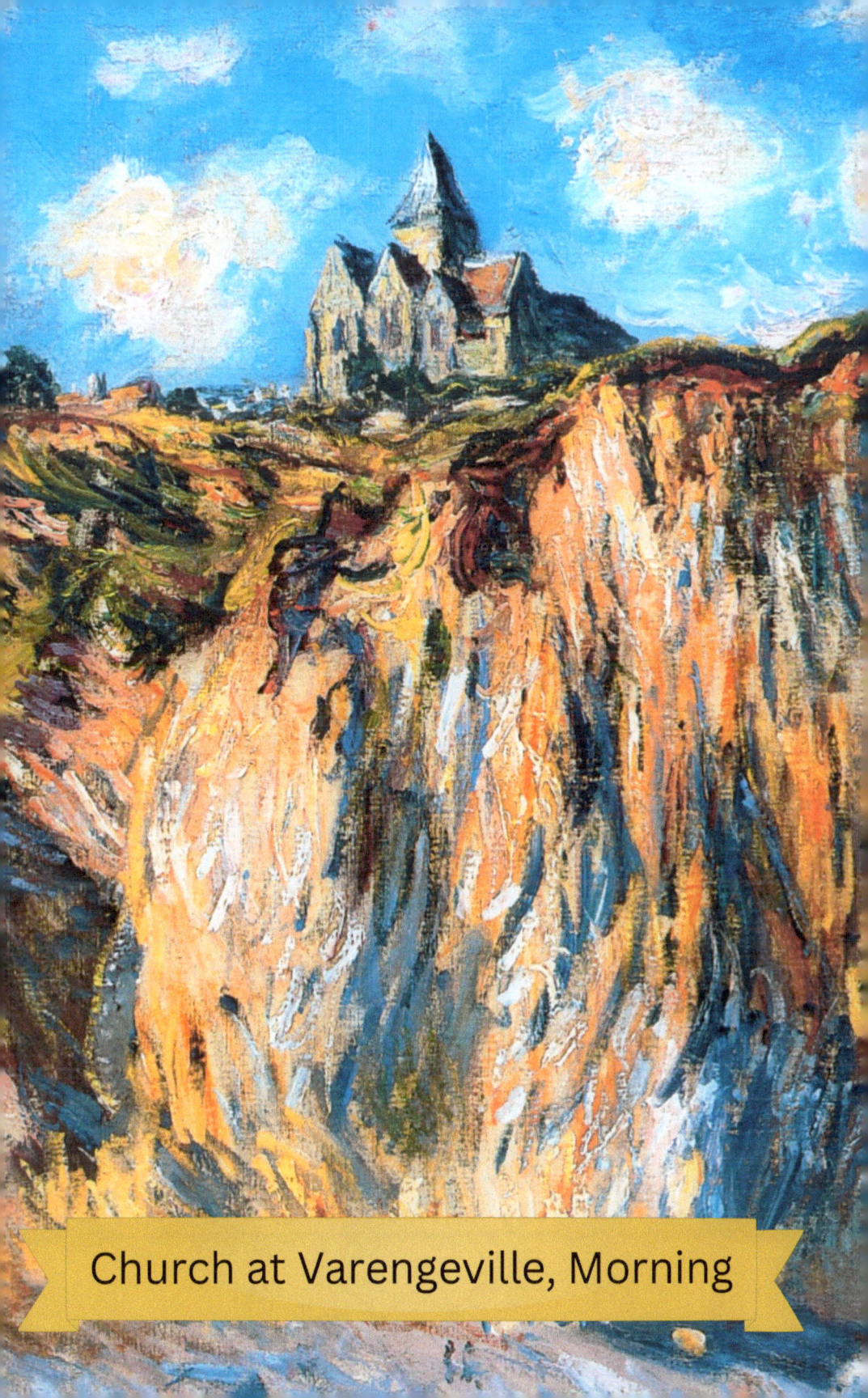
Church at Varengeville, Morning

Devote yourselves to prayer, being watchful and thankful.

Colossians 4:2

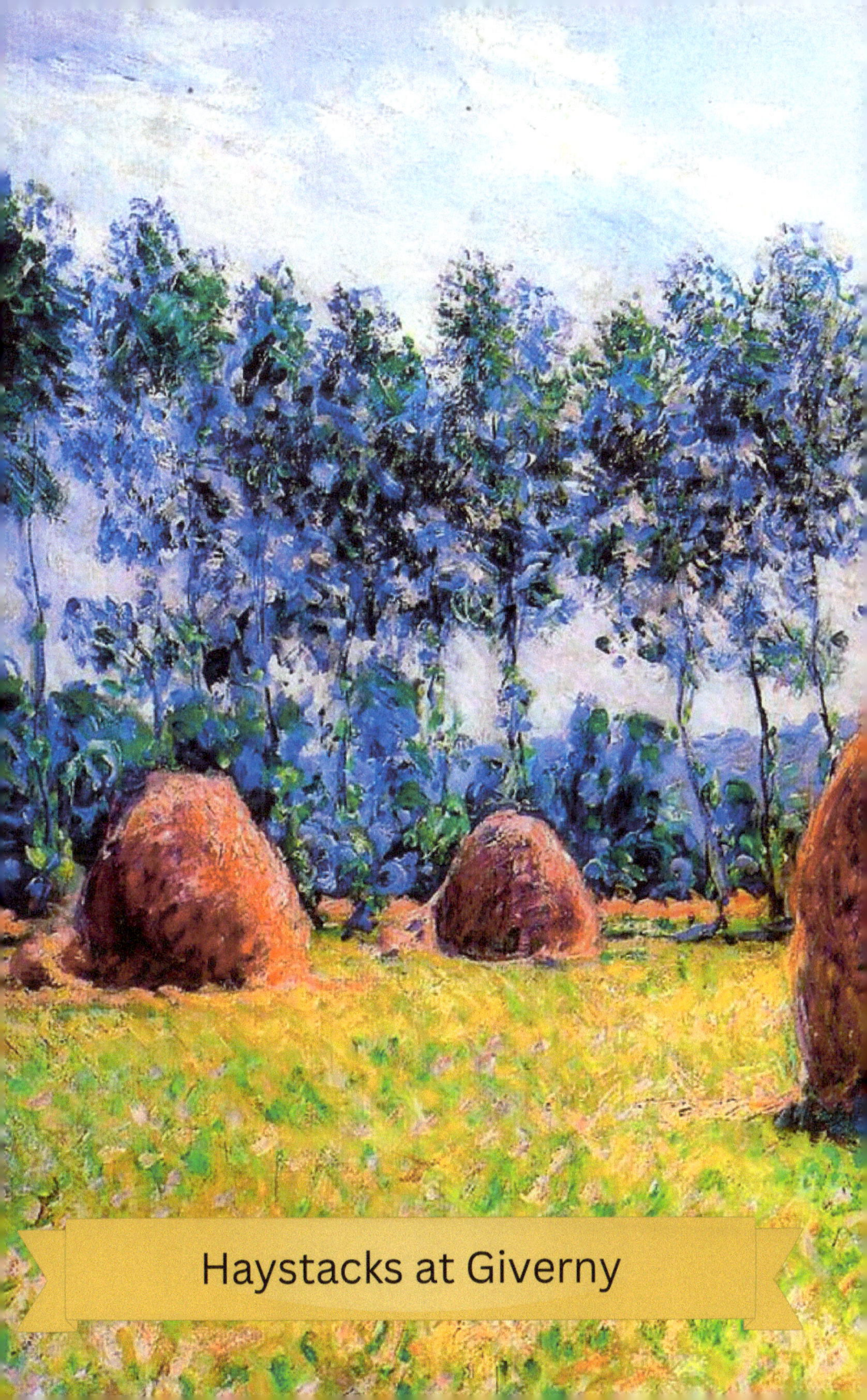
Haystacks at Giverny

so that from the rising of the sun to the place of its setting people may know there is none besides me. I am the LORD, and there is no other.

Isaiah 45:6

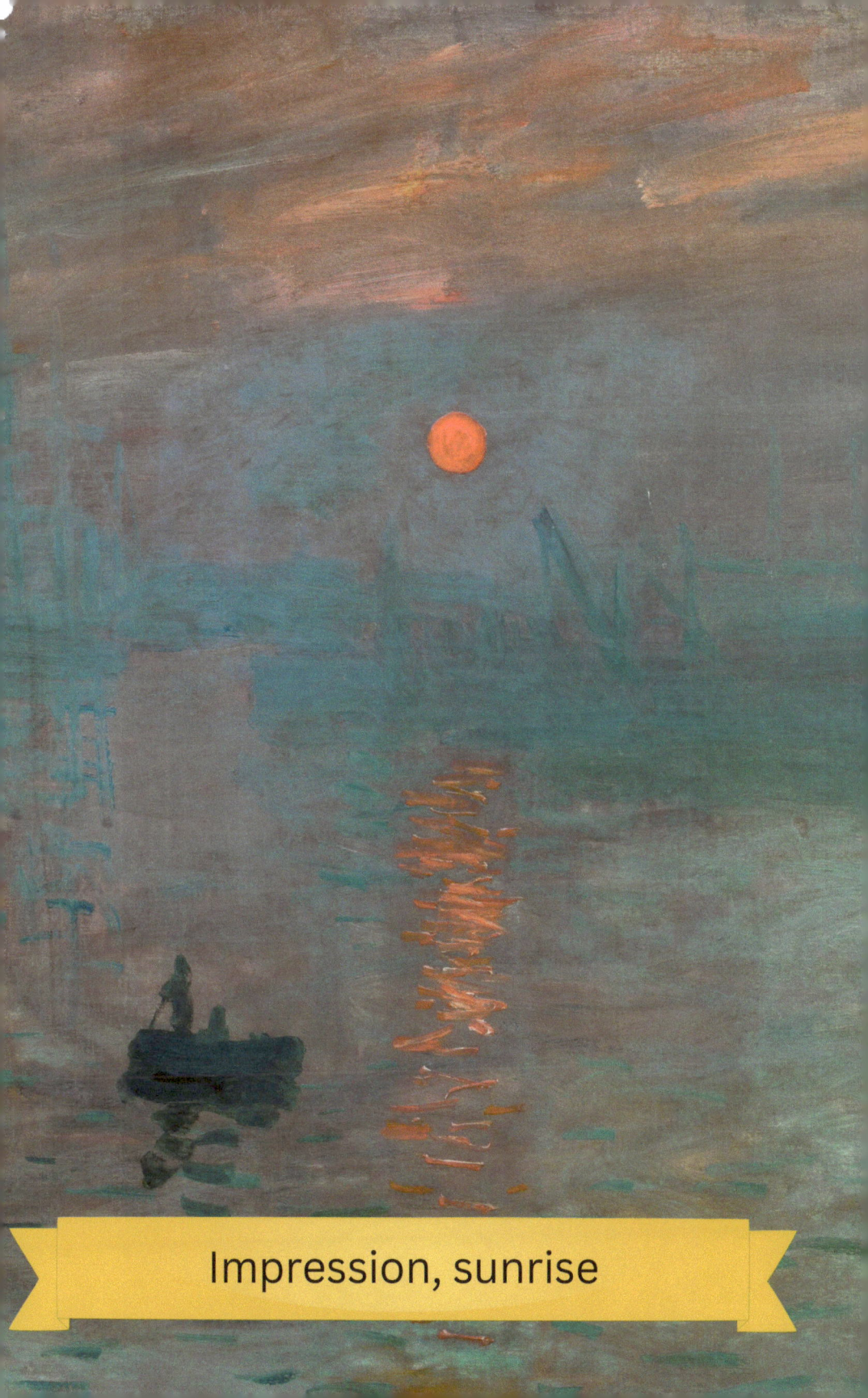
Impression, sunrise

Then you will call on me and come and pray to me, and I will listen to you.

Jeremiah 29:12

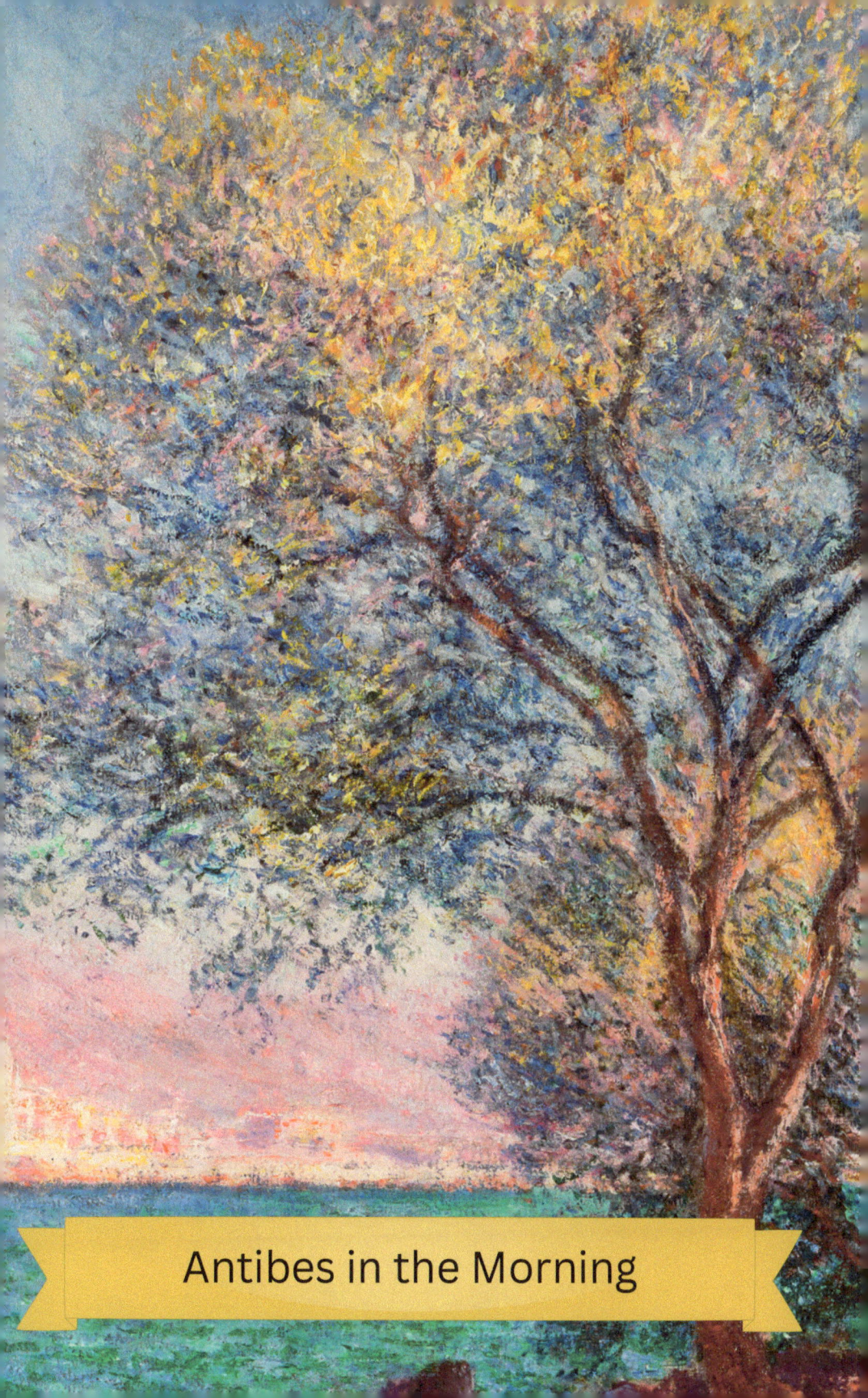
Antibes in the Morning

We love him, because he first loved us.

1 John 4:19

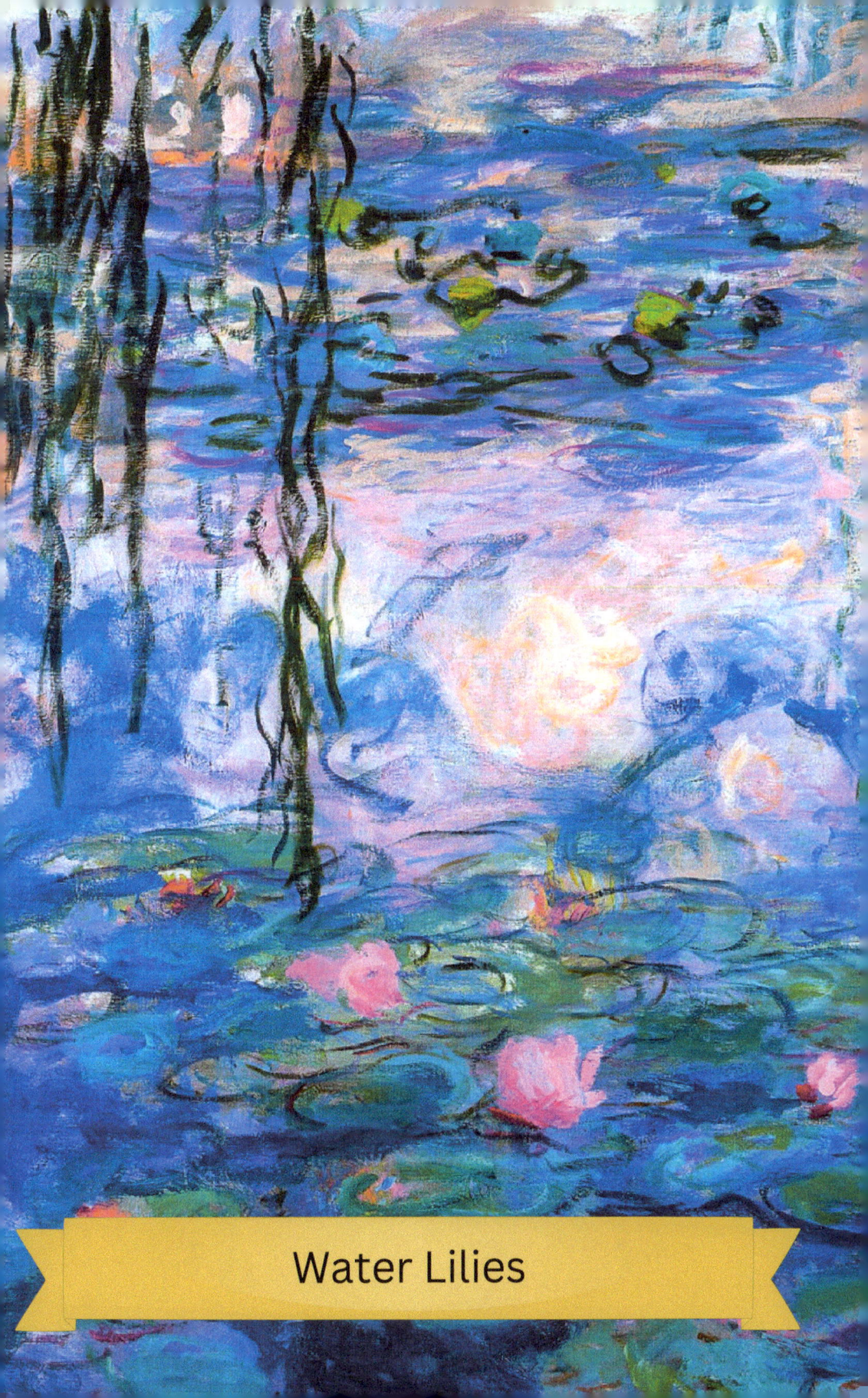

Water Lilies

A generous person will prosper; whoever refreshes others will be refreshed.

Proverbs 11:25

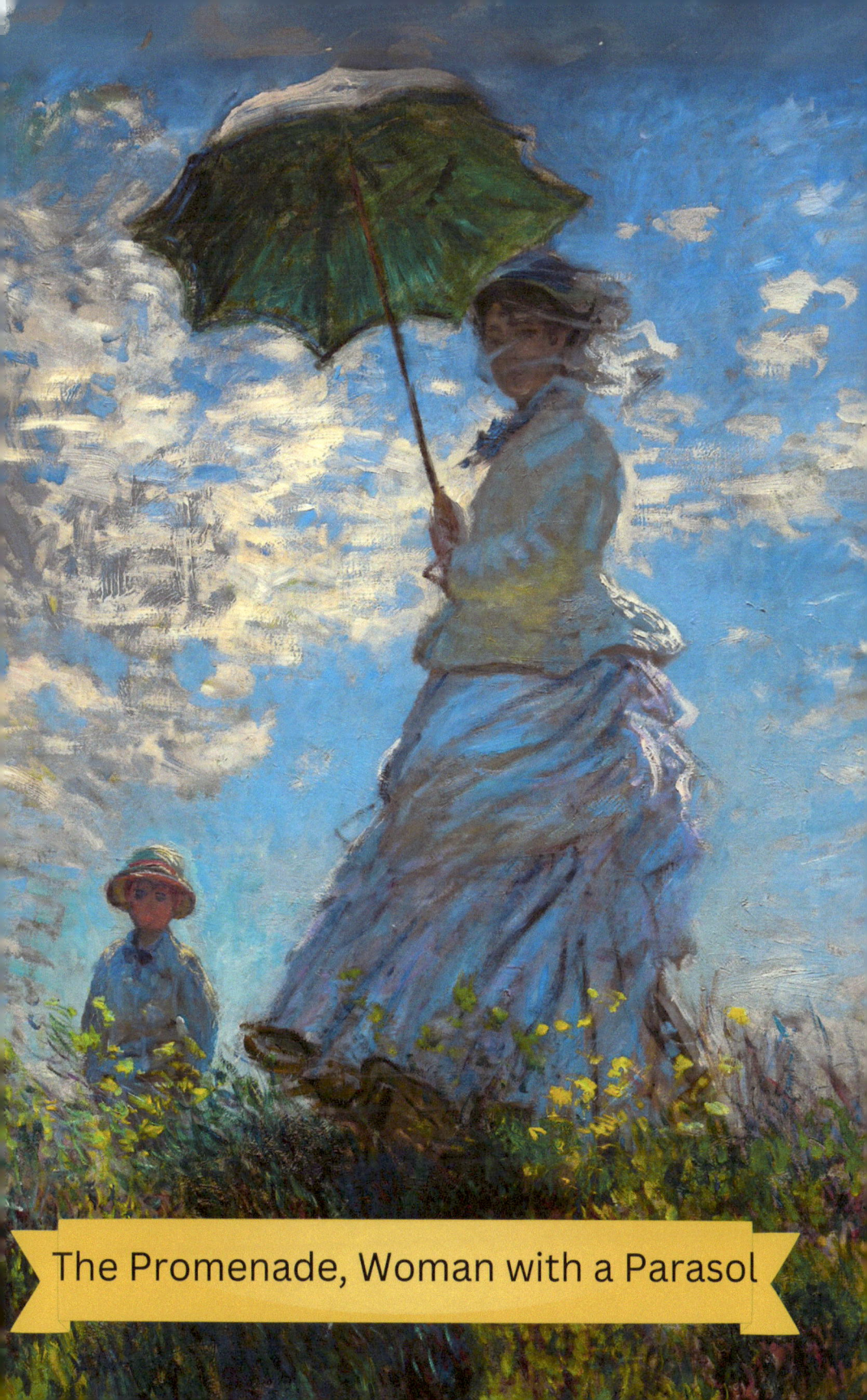
The Promenade, Woman with a Parasol

"For I know the plans I have for you," declares the Lord, "plans to prosper you and not to harm you, plans to give you hope and a future."

Jeremiah 29:11

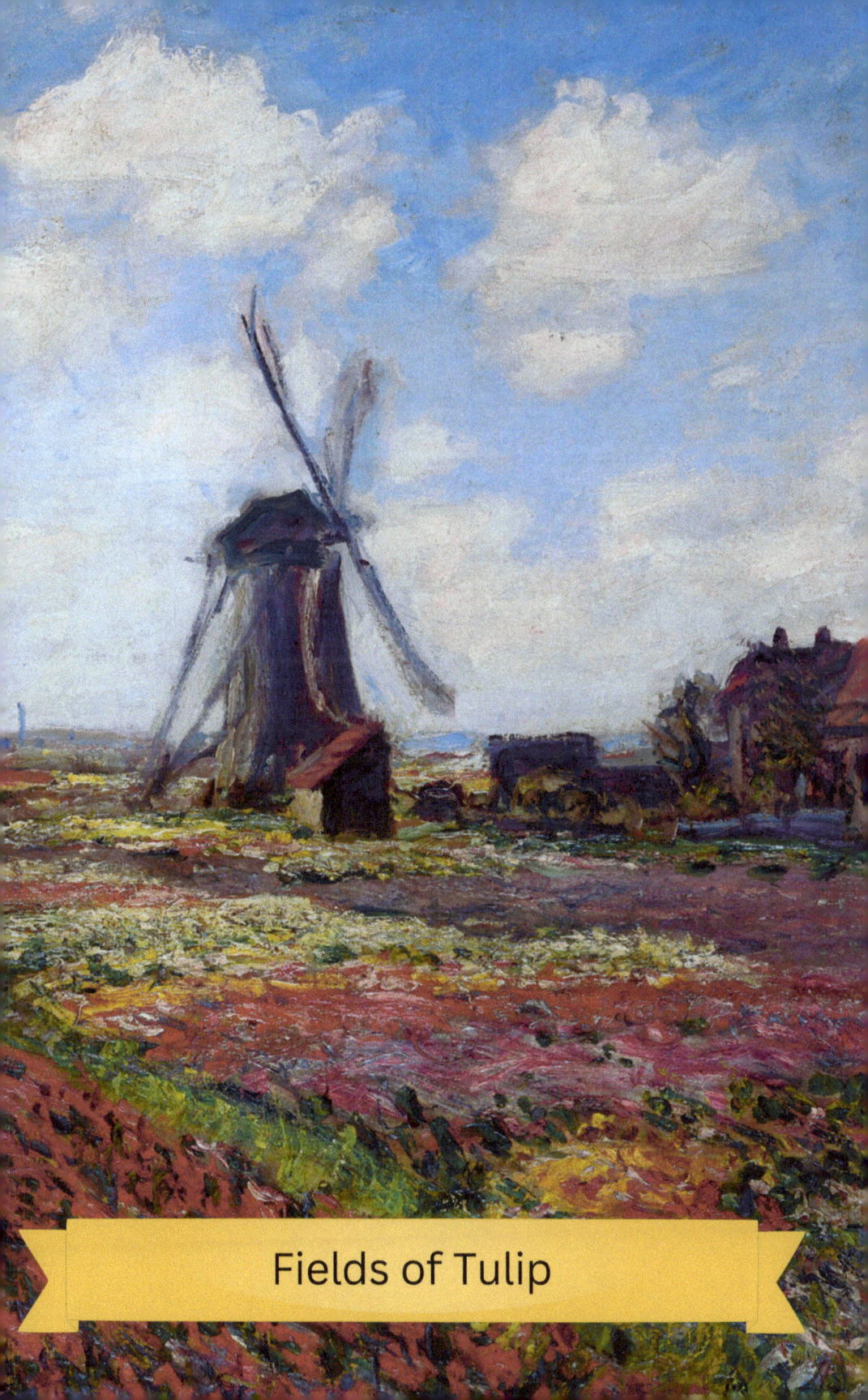
Fields of Tulip

The LORD will watch over your coming and going
both now and forevermore.

Psalm 121:8

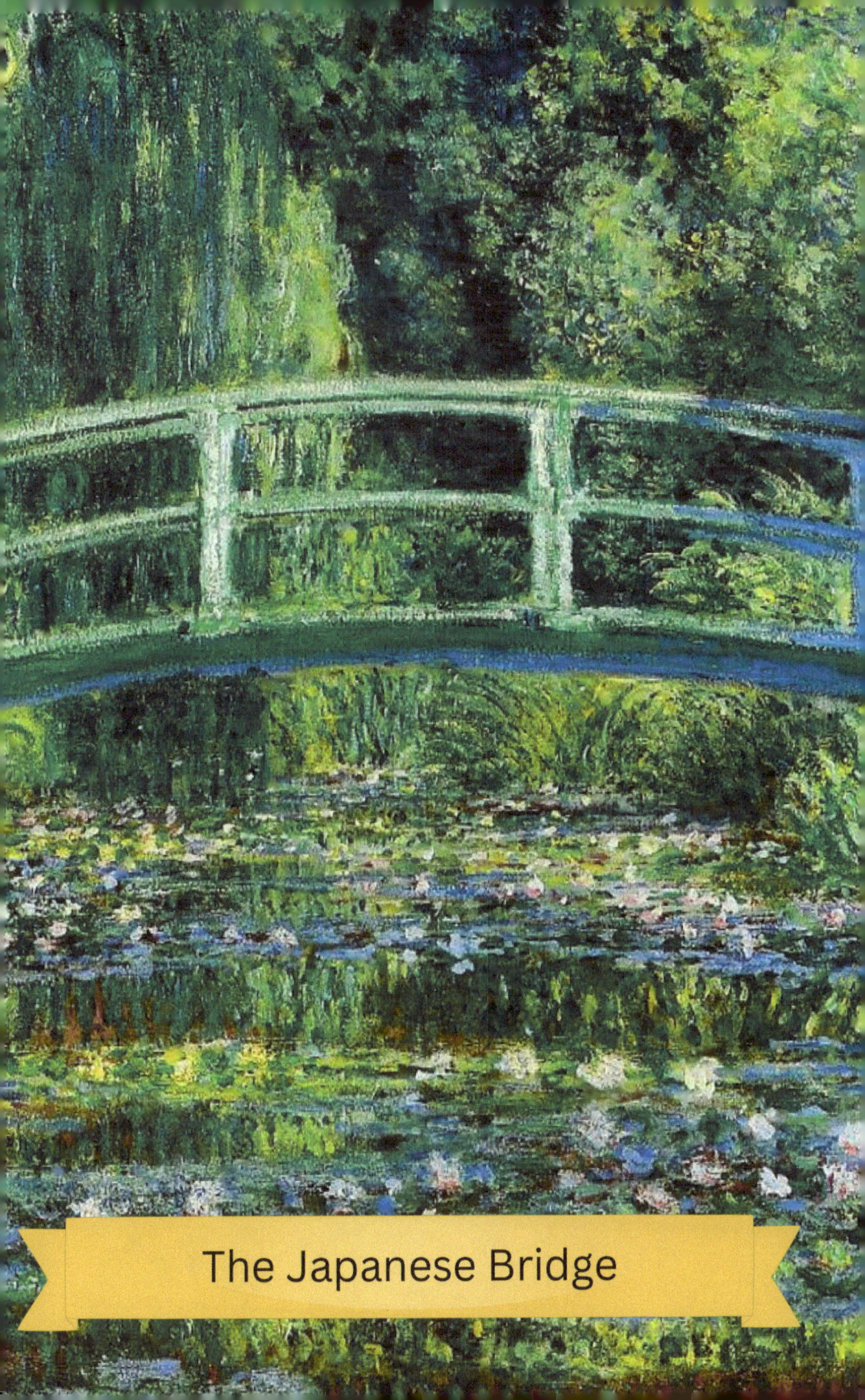

May the God of hope fill you with all joy and peace as you trust in him, so that you may overflow with hope by the power of the Holy Spirit.

Romans 15:13

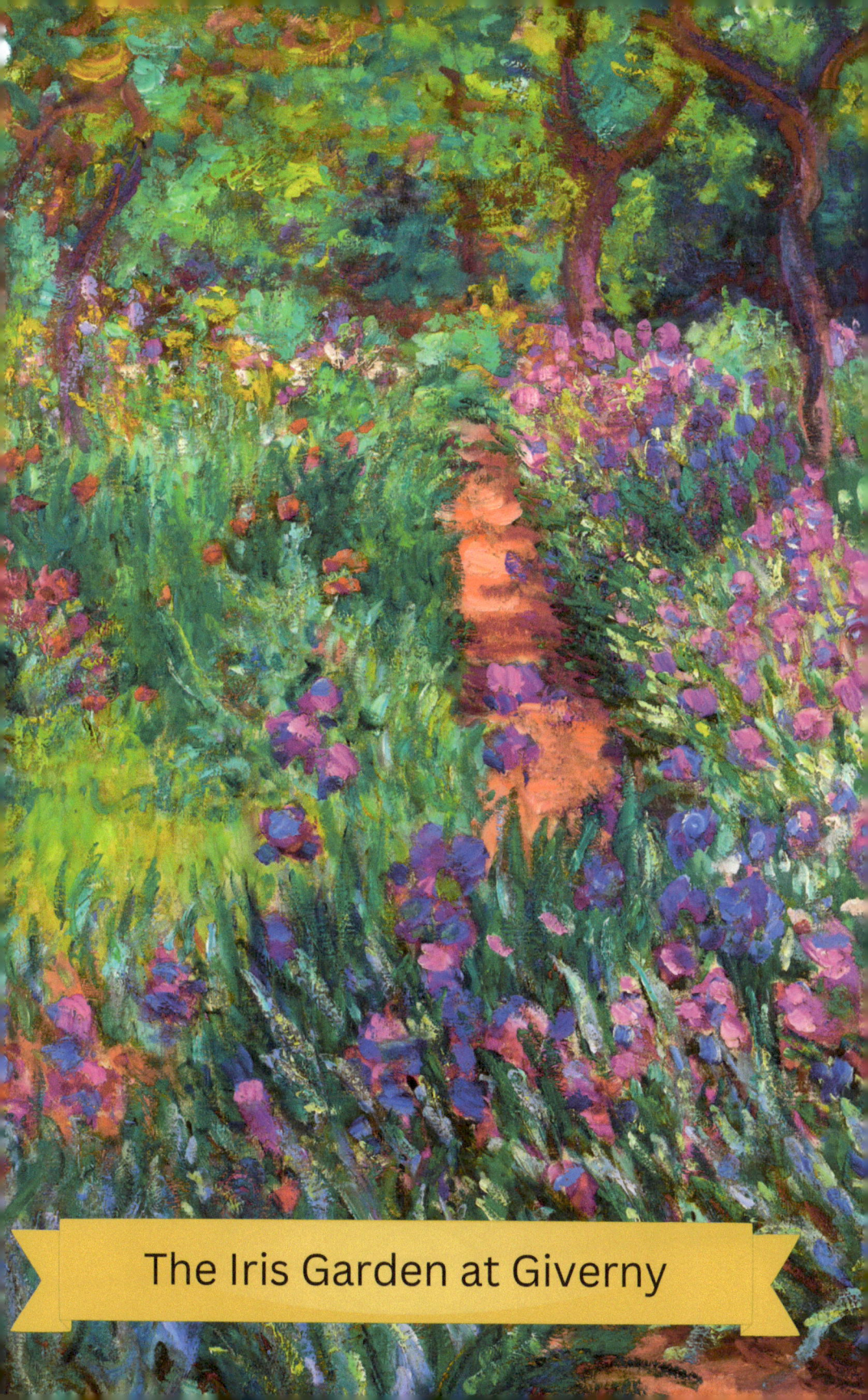
The Iris Garden at Giverny

Therefore I will look unto the LORD; I will wait for the God of my salvation: my God will hear me.

Micah 7:7

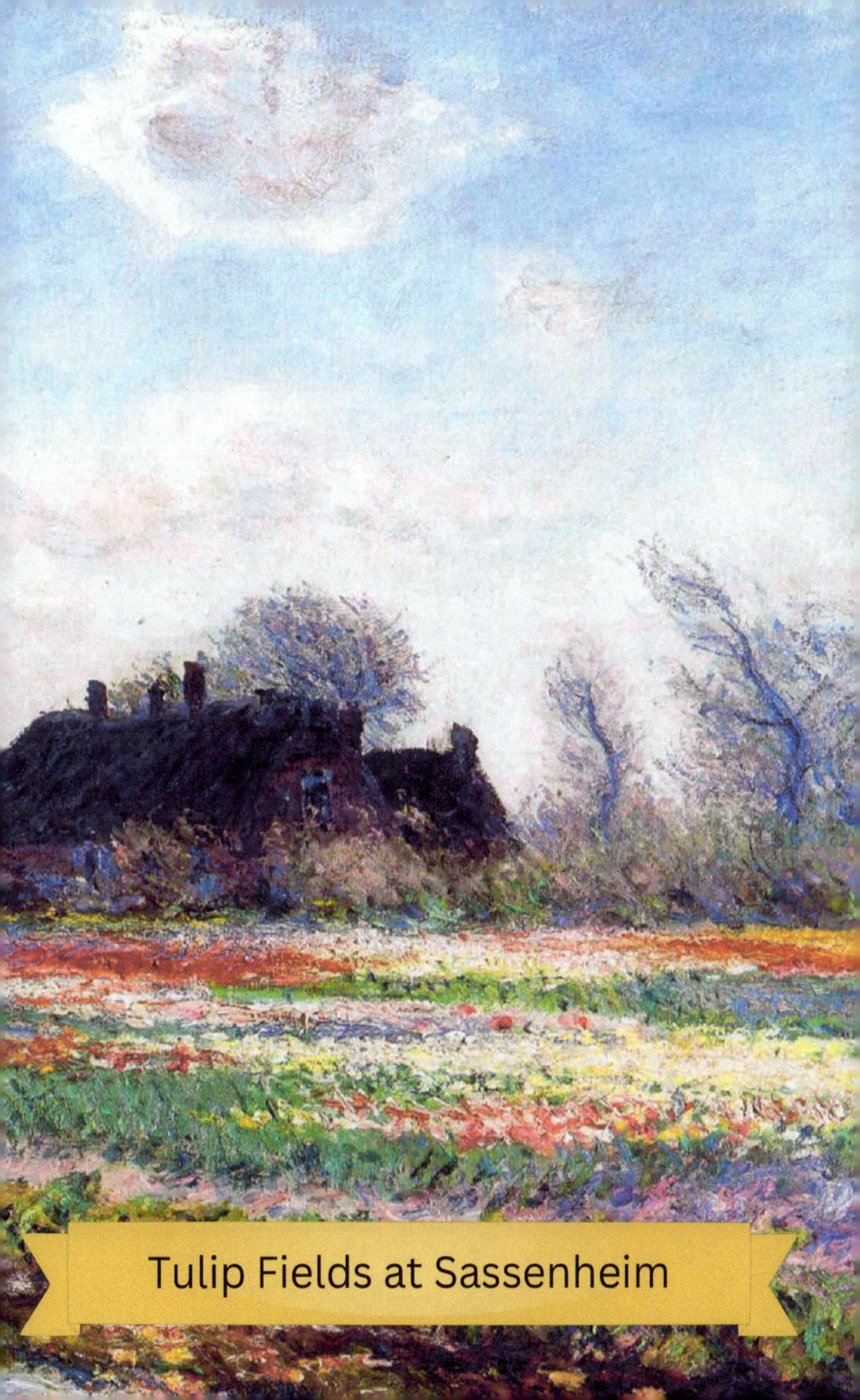
Tulip Fields at Sassenheim

Guide me in your
truth and
teach me,
for you are God
my Savior,
and my hope is in
you all day long.

Psalm 25:5